All Families

Single-Parent Families

by Elisa A. Bonnin

FOCUS READERS.

BEACON

www.focusreaders.com

Focus Readers is distributed by North Star Editions:
sales@northstareditions.com | 888-417-0195

Produced for Focus Readers by Red Line Editorial.

Photographs ©: Shutterstock Images, cover, 1, 6, 13, 14, 19, 22, 27; iStockphoto, 4, 8, 11, 16, 20–21, 25, 29

Library of Congress Cataloging-in-Publication Data
Names: Bonnin, Elisa A., author.
Title: Single-parent families / by Elisa A. Bonnin.
Description: Lake Elmo, MN : Focus Readers, [2023] | Series: All families | Includes index. | Audience: Grades 2-3
Identifiers: LCCN 2022030304 (print) | LCCN 2022030305 (ebook) | ISBN 9781637394601 (hardcover) | ISBN 9781637394977 (paperback) | ISBN 9781637395691 (ebook pdf) | ISBN 9781637395349 (hosted ebook)
Subjects: LCSH: Single-parent families--Juvenile literature. | Families--Juvenile literature.
Classification: LCC HQ759.915 .B66 2023 (print) | LCC HQ759.915 (ebook) | DDC 306.85/6--dc23/eng/20220628
LC record available at https://lccn.loc.gov/2022030304
LC ebook record available at https://lccn.loc.gov/2022030305

Printed in the United States of America
Mankato, MN
012023

About the Author

Elisa A. Bonnin was born and raised in the Philippines, after which she moved to the United States to study chemistry and later oceanography. After completing her doctorate, she moved to Germany to work as a postdoctoral scientist. She grew up in a single-parent family.

Table of Contents

Chapter 1

Father's Day

A girl's classmates are hard at work. Everyone in the room is drawing on cards. They are coloring pictures of themselves with their dads. The class is making cards for Father's Day.

 Art is an activity that helps children build skills as they grow up.

It's okay for big feelings to come up during school. Talking with trusted adults can help.

The girl doesn't know her dad. Her mom says he didn't want to live with them. So, the girl has never met him. She doesn't know how to draw his picture or where to send the card. She hasn't even started drawing.

Seeing this, her teacher comes up to her. The girl explains what's wrong. Her teacher smiles and says, "Why don't you make a card for your mom?"

The girl realizes it's okay to make a different card. She starts to draw.

Did You Know?

Eight out of ten kids in single-parent families live with their mom.

Chapter 2

Single Parents

Children live in single-parent families for lots of reasons. Sometimes, a parent dies. Some kids are born into a single-parent family. The other parent might not be involved in the child's life.

 When a parent dies, children need to grieve. Grieving means working through the pain over a loss.

There are many reasons why a parent might make that choice. A single parent can also **adopt** a child.

Some kids have two parents, but one parent does not live at home. A parent can get sent to prison. They stay in prison for their sentence. This can be a few months or many years.

Parents can also get a **divorce**. Or they can stop living together. Sometimes only one parent gets

custody. Other times, parents

share custody. But their kids still

live with one parent at a time.

Some kids mostly see one parent. The other parent might have to work in a different city. Or they may be sent to another country. Families can be apart for a long time.

Many parents are also in the military. People in the military can get deployed. They get sent

> During the 2010s, two million US children had a
> parent deployed to another country.

somewhere else. If that area is not

safe, their kids stay behind. The

other parent raises them at home.

Chapter 3

Challenges

Like all families, single-parent homes deal with challenges. Some single-parent families form when they lose a parent. That parent may have held a job. Without that job, money can be a challenge.

 Having enough money is a major worry for many adults.

▷ Taking music lessons can become too expensive for some families.

Having less money can have different **impacts**. For example, families might not be able to afford as many activities. Kids might feel sad about missing those activities.

Many single parents work extra jobs. That way, they earn more money. But parenting also involves other tasks. For example, parents cook meals and clean. They make sure their kids stay safe. They do all this work out of love.

This work means that most single parents are very busy. And being busy can make people tired. Feeling tired can make anger come more quickly. More anger can increase family arguments.

All these things impact children, too. Kids might feel **stress**. Stress can make people feel sad and angry. Sometimes, kids experience depression. This can last a long time. It often makes people feel deep sadness. They may also have little energy. These feelings can

Did You Know?

The United States has the highest number of single-parent families in the world.

 Many children in single-parent families become closer to their parents than other kids.

make school tougher. Students
might not be able to focus as well.

Some impacts can also be
positive. For instance, children in
single-parent families can be more
mature than other children.

Single Parents and Immigration

Moving to a new country can be complicated. Sometimes one parent is a **citizen**. The other is not. That parent needs **immigration papers**. And getting those papers can take many years. So, only one parent might be allowed to move. The family must wait for the other parent to come, too. For this reason, many immigrant families are also single-parent families. Children in these families don't know when they will see their other parent again. That experience can be very hard.

Millions of US children have at least one parent with no immigration papers.

EMPLOYMENT AUTHORIZATION
U.S. DEPARTMENT OF JUSTICE
Immigration and Naturalization Service
Name

PERMANENT RESIDENT CARD

A#
Birthdate
Category
Sex
M

UNITED STATES OF AMERICA

We recommend you use this envelope to protect your new card.

Nosotros recomendamos que usted use este sobre para proteger a su tarjeta.

Chapter 4

Meeting the Challenges

Single-parent families all face different struggles. A parent might leave or die. The child may feel sadness, anger, or confusion. They may feel all three. Sometimes, the parent wasn't safe to be around.

 Sometimes hugs can help people deal with really big feelings.

The child might feel better when that parent is gone. But the child might still miss the parent. All these feelings are okay.

Some children feel like their parent is gone because of them. A child might feel guilt or shame. However, the child didn't do anything wrong.

A parent might go to prison. People might say the parent was a bad person. But the child loves the parent anyway. The child might feel

 Big behaviors in class are often connected to experiences at home.

their love is wrong. But it is okay to love a parent who is in prison.

Big feelings can lead to big behaviors. For example, children might not follow rules at school. These can be hard times for kids.

They might need patient friends. Talking to adults can help, too.

Some children might be able to visit their parent. Or they might talk on the phone. These ways help children feel connected. If the parent died, children can still remember their parent. One way

 Memory boxes might include notes from a parent.

is with memory boxes. Children
fill the boxes. They might include
photos or clothing. That way, they'll
remember their parent forever.

FOCUS ON

Single-Parent Families

Write your answers on a separate piece of paper.

1. Write a few sentences describing different kinds of single-parent families.

2. Are you part of a single-parent family? If so, what is something you wish more people knew about? If not, what do you wish you knew?

3. What do parents often need when they move to a new country?
   - A. divorce
   - B. children in another country
   - C. immigration papers

4. How can having busy parents lead to challenges for families?
   - A. Busy parents have lots of extra time.
   - B. Busy parents never feel anger.
   - C. Busy parents are often more tired.

5. What does **sentence** mean in this book?

*They stay in prison for their **sentence**. This can be a few months or many years.*

    A. how long someone has to be in prison

    B. writing to family members

    C. a place to live

6. What does **deployed** mean in this book?

*People in the military can get **deployed**. They get sent somewhere else.*

    A. gaining a new parent

    B. sent somewhere for the military

    C. going on vacation

Answer key on page 32.

Glossary

adopt
To become the parent of a child who has other birth parents.

citizen
A person who is a legal member of a certain city or country.

custody
Having the legal right to take care of one's children.

divorce
A process where two people decide to stop being married.

immigration papers
The legal documents that people need to move to and stay in a different country.

impacts
Strong effects on a person or group.

mature
Acting grown-up or like an adult.

stress
The body and mind's responses to difficult situations.

To Learn More

BOOKS

Goozh, Judi, and Sue Jeweler. *Tell Me About When Moms and Dads Go to Jail*. Philadelphia: Jessica Kingsley Publishers, 2018.

Olsher, Sara. *What Happens When Parents Get Divorced?* Santa Rosa, CA: Mighty + Bright, 2021.

Swinton, Patty. *What's Life Like with a Single Parent?* New York: PowerKids Press, 2019.

NOTE TO EDUCATORS

Visit **www.focusreaders.com** to find lesson plans, activities, links, and other resources related to this title.

Index

Answer Key: 1. Answers will vary; **2.** Answers will vary; **3.** C; **4.** C; **5.** A; **6.** B